Creative Dough Crafts

100 Delightful Designs to Make in Your Own Kitchen

▪ Brigitte Casagranda ▪

Lark Books

Editor: Holly Boswell
Translated from the French by Mark Clifton, Translations Plus
Production: Elaine Thompson

Library of Congress Catalog-in-Publication Data
Casagranda, Brigitte.
    Creative dough crafts : 100 delightful designs to make in your own
kitchen / Brigitte Casagranda.
        p.   cm.
    Includes index.
    ISBN 1-887374-49-3
    1. Bread dough craft.   I. Title.
TT880.C34   1997
745.5--dc21   97-25164
                                                                    CIP

10 9 8 7 6 5 4 3 2 1

First Edition

Published by Lark Books
50 College Street
Asheville, NC 28801
USA

© 1997 Lark Books

First published in France under the titles

  Petits metiers en pate a sel
  © 1994 Dessain et Tolra, Paris

  Contes et metiers en pate a sel
  © 1992 Dessain et Tolra, Paris

  Pate a sel, meubles de poupees
  © 1994 Dessain et Tolra, Paris

  Pate a sel, decors de table
  © 1995 Dessain et Tolra, Paris

  Noel en pate a sel
  © 1994 Dessain et Tolra, Paris

Distributed by Random House, Inc., in the United States, Canada,
    the United Kingdom, Europe, and Asia

Distributed in Australia by Capricorn Link (Australia) Pty Ltd.,
    P. O. Box 6651, Baulkham Hills Business Centre, NSW 2153, Australia

Distributed in New Zealand by Tandem Press Ltd., 2 Rugby Rd.,
    Birkenhead, Auckland, New Zealand

Printed in Hong Kong by H & Y Printing Ltd.

ISBN 1-887374-49-3

CONTENTS

Basic Techniques

RECIPE

For all the creations presented in this book, I have used a natural dough without any leavening agent, composed of:

2 cups of flour
1 cup of fine salt
1 cup of water (or less)

Using these proportions, you can complete any project given in this book.

SALT

Choose a fine grain, non-iodized, non-fluoridated table salt. It's the easiest to work with.

FLOUR

Choose the most ordinary all-purpose flour that is the least expensive, and stick with the brand. Keep a good stock on hand.

WATER

Use cold water, and add it slowly to the salt and flour mixture.

To prepare the dough you will need:

1 large mixing bowl
1 cup
1 wooden spoon
Flour
Water
Salt

Mix two cups of flour and one cup of salt in the mixing bowl, then make a hollow in the middle and slowly pour in a cup of water.

Use a wooden spoon to mix well until you form a ball. If your work space is warmer than 70°F (21°C), the dough will become too soft and difficult to model.

Sift flour over a working surface and work the dough as long as necessary to obtain a smooth ball, well mixed and without any lumps. If the dough crumbles, add water. If it sticks to your fingers, add flour.

Knead the dough so it is flexible and has a manageable consistency, preferably with both hands deeply working in the dough.

You should now have a lukewarm, manageable saltdough ready to model.

As you find the exact proportions that work best for you, record them for future use.

PRESERVING THE DOUGH

It is recommended that the saltdough leftovers be stored in a sealed container, or better yet in plastic wrap or a zip-lock bag. Place it in a cool space, but not the refrigerator.

Your modeling dough will be easiest to work if you prepare it the same day you will use it. As time passes, it loses its elasticity and flexibility.

EQUIPMENT

To model your saltdough creations, you should have the following utensils available around your working surface:

Rolling pin	Forming chisels
Kitchen knife	Steel wire
Water glass to mix repair paste	Wire cutters
	Aluminum foil
Pastry brush	Flour
Drinking straw	Tea strainer
Toothpicks	
Garlic press	

WORKING SURFACE

Choose a smooth surface (such as Formica) that is easy to clean with a sponge or a plastic coated cloth.

You will notice that it is easier to model with clean hands. Rinse your hands often to remove the dried saltdough from your fingers and palms.

MODELING

All saltdough is done in small scale—hand size, in fact. The easiest approach is to do your modeling on a sheet of aluminum foil, or on a foil-covered baking sheet. Most saltdough is baked on aluminum foil, at least for the first half of the total baking time. If you start on the foil, you won't have to move the figures after you've finished, possibly distorting their shape in the process. For many projects, the foil will be removed halfway through baking, when the figures have hardened somewhat and can be placed directly on the oven rack. See individual project instructions.

JOINING

Every time you add a new piece of dough, moisten it lightly, using a pastry brush, or a spray bottle.

Always moisten only the surfaces to be joined. Excess water can distort the modeling and increase baking time.

Keep your working surface and your equipment clean. Have a moist sponge, a cloth, flour, and a glass of water within reach.

The leftover saltdough can be kept for 24 hours in plastic wrap or a sealed container. If the dough should become too moist, you will be able to re-work it by adding flour until it again has a good consistency, smooth and flexible to the touch.

BAKING

I usually bake between 200°F (100°C) and 250°F (125°C). Unless the piece is much thinner or thicker than usual, these are the temperatures indicated throughout this book. A gas or electric oven is ideal, as long as you follow the baking times and the temperatures given. Some gas ovens require as little as half the time that electric ovens do. To test for dryness, tap your index finger on the piece. It should sound like hardened clay rather than giving off a dull thud.

If the oven door is left slightly ajar the first hour of baking, the humidity will escape more readily and the pieces will dry more efficiently.

Air-drying and sun-drying also work well but take longer. Allow about a day for every $\frac{1}{16}$" (0.15 cm) thickness of dough.

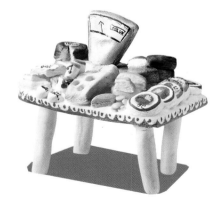

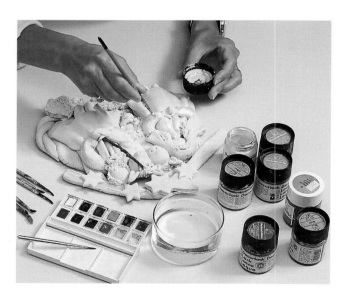

FINISHING

Before painting, brush away the excess flour. If necessary, use sandpaper to smooth the piece, or scrape with a knife, then remove all grit and dust.

Remove the rough edges with a scraper or knife so as to get a well-finished product.

PAINTING

Simple saltdough projects can be left the lovely warm color of baked bread, especially if they are varnished (see page 10). On the other hand, for most of the projects in this book, painting is just as important as modeling.

A variety of paints work well on saltdough: acrylics, watercolors, inks, and gouaches. If you've always wanted to play with these "artist's" paints, saltdough is the perfect place to start. You'll also need good-quality brushes in a variety of sizes, from very fine (for painting lines) to broader ones that will allow you to cover a large surface efficiently.

Start at the beginning: observe, paint, observe again, note the effect—and persevere! If you make a mistake, you can always pass a lightly moistened sponge over the work and dry it with a clean cloth. Once the dough is dry, you can start over.

One final tip: if you want very bright, vibrant color, give the baked dough figure a white primer coat. Allow to dry before you paint the project in your chosen colors.

HANGERS

Your creation can be hung, as long as a hook of steel wire, formed in the shape of a hairpin, is inserted before or when baking is half done. Then you can suspend it with a ribbon whose colors match those of your creation after painting and varnishing.

In themselves, these creations are often like small primitive paintings. If you wish, you can frame them with a little picture frame or a ready-made mat found in framing shops, or made at home using natural or painted molding.

Saltdough also adheres to cork, burlap, or linen cloth. You can make your own compositions.

REPAIRS

Gluing a work that is not yet painted is easy. Make a paste by grinding or pounding dried saltdough crumbs into powder, and adding a little water. Then apply it to the pieces to be rejoined. Bake again until it has set. When a hand or a foot is broken, it is possible to remodel a new one and attach it by moistening it lightly. Bake it again. Smooth with sandpaper as necessary.

To glue a work that has already been painted and varnished, you can use wood glue, or fast-drying glue. Then repaint and revarnish, as necessary. This works if it's not too broken.

If the modeled work is really damaged, you can fill in the damage with paste and let it air dry. Once dry, sand and repaint. Afterward you can revarnish it.

Liquid saltdough

VARNISHING

This is indispensable! It is preferable to select a varnish that is the same brand as your paint.

Varnish gives vividness to the colors and also assures a better preservation of your creations by protecting them from dust.

After the piece is thoroughly dry, apply two or three coats, always drying between coats.

If you select a wood varnish, even a colorless one, it will yellow the saltdough somewhat. Marine varnishes are transparent and glossy. Polyurethane is excellent. To be extra sure, you can experiment on some saltdough test samples.

Set your varnished work to dry on wooden toothpicks or craft sticks, so drying can take place above and below without sticking.

Don't forget to dip your brushes in mineral spirits. Then wash them in warm water with soap. Rinse them well, then dry them with a cloth.

DECORATING

ACCESSORIES

Small mirror
Pieces of glass such as
microscope slides
Wood chips
Natural moss
Newspaper
Tissue paper
Lace and braid
String
Wood glue

NATURAL MATERIALS

Birdseed
Wood chips
Moss
Dried flowers
Pieces of wood
Juniper berry seeds
Star-shaped anise seeds
Cloves

Keep the above accessories within reach,
as you may need them during modeling.

After varnishing a piece completely, you can
add elements to decorate your creation using
a good wood glue, or a quick setting glue.

If you insert any pieces of wood, make sure
they are well dried.

Shells and pebbles provide extra volume, and
a new material to saltdough. You must press
seeds sufficiently deep into the saltdough that
they don't come loose after baking.

Glass and mirrors can take the heat as long
as it does not exceed 200°F (100°C). It is
preferable not to include too large a piece.

Glue on elements such as wood chips, dried
flowers or moss after varnishing.

For the Nursery

THE SAND MAN

"You, you alone, will have the stars as no one else has them..."
"What are you trying to say?"
"When you look at the sky, at night, since I will be living in one of them. In one of them I shall be laughing. And so it will be as if all the stars were laughing, when you look at the sky at night ... You, only you, will have stars that know how to laugh"...
(The Little Prince,
by Antoine de Saint-Exupéry).

Shape the clouds and stars (see below) and join them. The moon connects these shapes together. Model the sand man and his sack as depicted in the photo. His hair is strained through a garlic press. Make holes for nylon thread to dangle pendants.

Bake on foil at 200°F (100°C) for 1 hour, then remove foil and bake at 250°F (125°C) for 2 hours.

Cut out stars with a cookie cutter.

Make small holes before baking.

Bake the stars at 165°F (75°C) for 1 hour. Sprinkle glitter sparingly over varnish while still wet.

BABY MEDALLIONS

To view the finished medallions, turn to page 15.

Roll the dough ¼" (.5 cm) thick. Cut out a circle using a cookie cutter.

Using a straw, make two holes through which to thread a ribbon after baking.

Form a pillow and arrange it on the circle, slightly moistening it first.

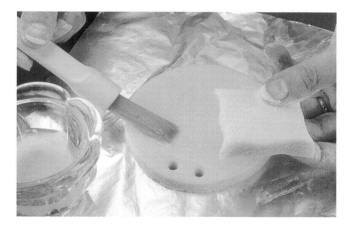

Shape a baby (complete with head and body) and place it with its head on the pillow.

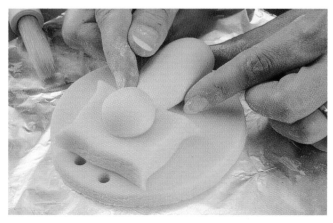

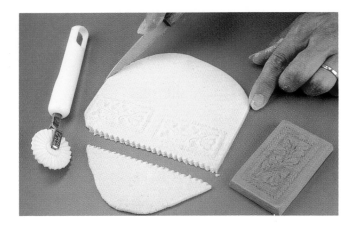

Roll out dough thinly to make the sheet or blanket. Decorate it by pressing a raised stamp into the surface.

Cover the baby with the blanket, and fold back the top.

Make the hair by pressing dough through a sieve, then attach it with a knife. Position the arms and hands as you want them. Bake at 200°F (100°C) for 2 hours.

BABY MAUVE

Space some berries regularly along the edge of the sheet, and add a spray of berries on each side of the pillow.

BABY ROSE

Place flowers and leaves on the folded down portions of the sheet and on each side of the pillow.

The sleeping baby mice below were shaped much like the human babies on the previous pages. The mother mouse—clearly English—and her cottage illustrate the whimsey that salt-dough seems to invite.

ROCKING HORSES

This rocking horse is made ⅜"
(1 cm) thick, and can serve as a
guide for creating other ponies.
In flat pieces such as this one, the
dough can rise, distorting your
design. If the surface of the horse
puffs up, you can, at mid-baking,
push down the blistered surface
using a glove, and continue the
baking at a lower temperature.

LITTLE PONIES

These ponies are cut out with a cookie cutter. It's up to you whether to add a rocking base. With a large number of ponies, you could create a mobile for a child's room, or Christmas tree ornaments. Make a hole to hang them with colored string or ribbon.

Roll out the saltdough very thinly. Cut a rectangle, and fringe both ends with a knife.

🕐 Careful! The rugs are not very thick, consequently, baking must not be too high or too long. Baking at 165°F (75°C) for 1 hour is sufficient.

Even if the modeling of a rug is very simple, baking it does raise some problems. It must be watched constantly. If a bubble raises the surface of the rug, the whole process must be started over.

Decorating the rugs is the best part. Match the tones, and the motifs, with the furniture of the room in which you will place the rug, just as you do for your own interior. The most surprising juxtapositions work well as long as they are carefully thought out. You will find several examples of rugs throughout this chapter.

Spread out the saltdough and cut out the oval, rectangle, or circle which will serve as a supportive frame for the mirror.

Place a mirror in the center of the saltdough frame, pressing it slightly so as to create the mirror frame. You should refine and work this with a knife point.

Decorate the frame with leaves, flowers, or with a simple, traditional border, imitating a molding.

Bake the entire work at 200°F (100°C) for 1 hour.

Then paint the mirror frame. Acrylic paints with various gold tones give your mirror an elegant style. To avoid any incompatibility between the paint and the varnish, consult with your supplier.

First, model the ceramic tile wall. Roll out a rectangle of saltdough, then score it vertically and horizontally.

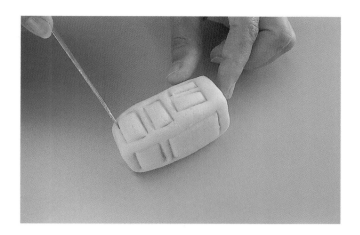

Now model the stove, using a knife to score the different drawers and burner lids.

 Bake for 10 minutes at 200°F (100°C).

While the stove is baking, model the vent stack, the metal bar for the front of the stove, the shelves, the log holder, the saucepans, the cooking utensils, etc.

Bake all the elements for 10 minutes at 200°F (100°C).

Then place the stove on the ceramic wall. To make it stick, moisten the adjoining surfaces and add some saltdough paste with a pastry brush. Then set the stack and metal bar in place, joining them the same way.

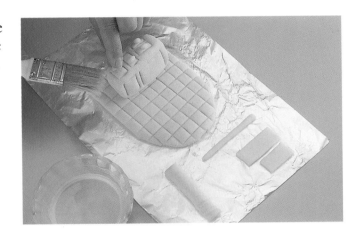

Install the shelves with the crockery. Add the log holder, slightly hollowed out, and prick it with a fork. Always moisten with the pastry brush every element you add.

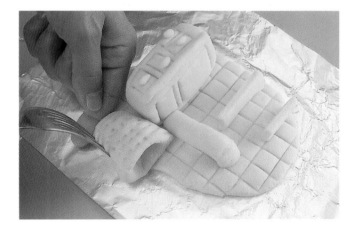

When all the elements are assembled, place everything in the oven for 1 hour at 200°F (100°C), but no longer since there is a risk the tile wall might rise. After baking for 1 hour, bring the temperature to 250°F (125°C) and bake another 2 hours, as this model is relatively thick.

Wire tiny bundles of twigs together for the kindling (willow twigs are shown), using brass wire. Place one bundle in the log holder and lay the rest by the stove.

Spread out a rectangle of salt dough, and score it vertically and horizontally, so as to outline the ceramic tiles and the beams. Use the tip of the knife to model the hanging plates. Cut out the window, leaving a vertical and a horizontal cross-piece.

Model the wash basin and bake it for 1 hour at 200°F (100°C). Then place it on the bottom of the window segment, slightly moistened with the pastry brush, and bake both pieces together for 2 hours at 250°F (125°C).

This model requires lots of decoration with acrylic paint. Varnish the whole project with a matte colorless acrylic varnish. Choose a fine lace, slightly starched, and iron it making several folds. Cut the lace to the window width. Glue the lace to the window with wood glue, or a quick setting glue.

Roll out your saltdough. Cut out the elements of the sofa: seat ¼" (0.6 cm) thick, the back (a little less thick), and the rounded armrests. Model the four feet.

🕐 Bake all the pieces 10 minutes at 200°F (100°C), then assemble them. Insert wooden toothpicks in the feet so you can attach them to the sofa body. Bake the sofa for 1 hour at 200°F (100°C). Add a few cushions of salt-dough which you model during this time. Bake the whole assembly again, this time for 1 hour at 250°F (125°C).

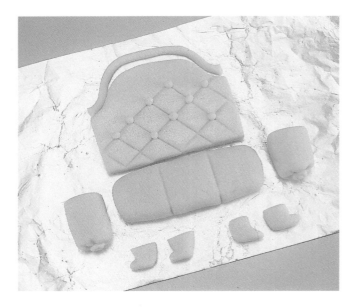

THE ARMCHAIR

Roll out your saltdough. Cut out and model the elements: the seat ¼" (0.6 cm) thick, the back, the two armrests, the four feet.

The assembly and baking are the same as for the sofa.

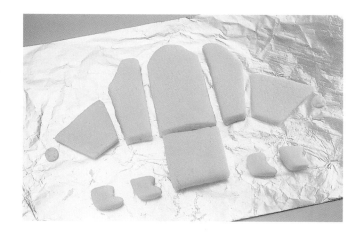

THE LAMP

Model the base of the lamp. Insert a toothpick into the base and attach a ball of saltdough for the bulb.

Roll out a small piece of saltdough and finely notch it for the shade.

🕐 Place the lampshade on aluminum foil and bake it for 10 minutes at 200°F (100°C).

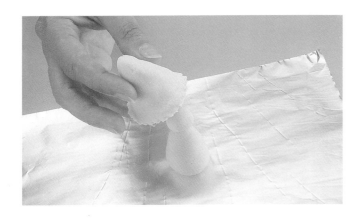

Join the two elements, after having delicately removed the aluminum foil from inside the lampshade.

THE FIREPLACE

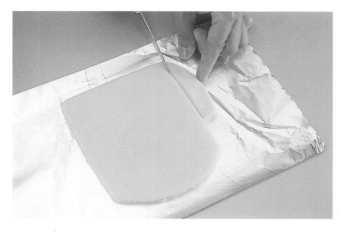

Follow the same steps used for modeling the stove (pages 24 and 25).

Roll out the dough, then cut out the wall, which will serve as a support. Keep a small additional piece on one side, attached to the wall, which will form the trunk of the decorative tree.

In the center, place a rectangle of saltdough. This is the fireplace; sculpt it with a pointed knife. Remove the center, into which, after baking and varnishing, you will insert small pieces of wood.

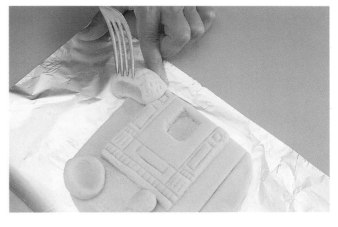

Embellish the top of the fireplace and wall with vases, plates, a mirror, a picture, or any other object which suits your fancy.

Add a log basket. Hollow it out and prick it using the tines of a fork.

Cut out some leaves from flat saltdough. Place them along the tree trunk.

Bake the entire piece once for 1 hour at 200°F (100°C) to avoid any swelling, then 1 hour at 250°F (125°C), for a total baking time of 2 hours.

Cut out the vanity top in the form of a kidney bean.

🕐 Bake it for 10 to 15 minutes at 200°F (100°C) so that it stays good and flat (a higher temperature will make it warp).

Create a thick support of aluminum foil on which you will lay the top.

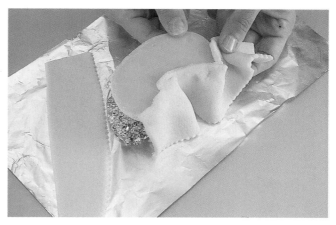

Cut out a strip of saltdough, notch it with a pastry roller, and gather it around the hollow part of "the bean", pressing against the aluminum reinforcement.

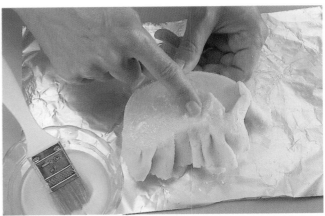

Create a second layer of skirt with notched edging, and place it as indicated.

After having lightly moistened the edge of the skirting, place it on the edge of the top. Press firmly but delicately with a finger. This is detailed work.

 Bake the piece for 1 hour at 200°F (100°C).

Carefully remove the aluminum foil reinforcement, and bake again for 1 hour at the same temperature.

THE STOOL

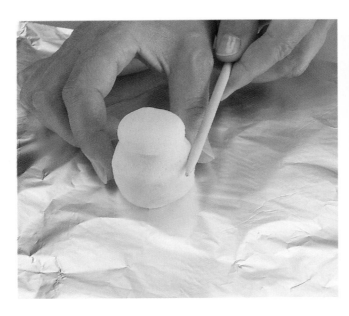

Model a shape resembling a champagne cork.

Cut out two strips of saltdough, notch the edges, and wrap them around the stool.

 Bake it at 212°F (100°C) for 10 minutes.

 Then bake it at 200°F (100°C) for 1 hour.

First, create the mattress by cutting it from a relatively wide strip of saltdough ¼" (0.6 cm) thick.

To make a bolster, roll up a sheet of saltdough, jellyroll style. (This is the best way to make "ropes," or strands, of dough for just about any project, including the wreaths in the Christmas section.) Put the bolster at the head of the bed.

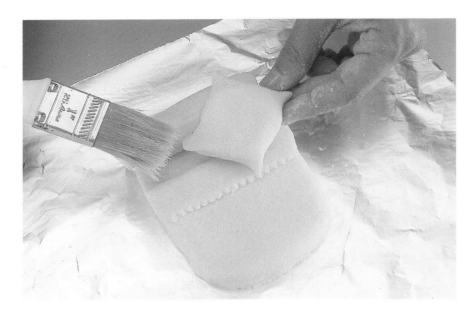

For the sheet and the coverlet, cut out a thin piece of flat saltdough. Fold it, notch it, and place it as shown.

Form and place the pillows.

Partially bake them all together.

Prepare the headboard, then the four legs into which toothpicks are inserted.

Bake the bed with the headboard for 1 hour and 30 minutes at 200°F (100°C), then fasten the legs to the bed and bake again at 250°F (125°C) for 30 minutes.

Model a rectangular form ¼"-⅜" (0.6-1 cm) thick. Use a knife point to trace the doors, the lock, and any carved designs. Add some balls of saltdough for the knobs, and balls for the chest's feet.

Make the lid from a wide flat strip of salt-dough.

Modeling a chest is simple. This form lends itself to variations of imaginative, decorative painting. After baking 1 hour at 200°F (100°C), you can decorate the lid and the chest with twin motifs, such as initials. A garland of flowers can embellish the chest base or its lid and sides. A simpler motif can decorate the feet. For more delicacy in tracing the motifs, paint flowers, stems, leaves, and scrolls freehand, with a fine # 2 brush.

Although armoires can vary with every taste, they are constructed the same basic way (see page 42).

A blue and white armoire with leaves and flowers

*A pink and
blue armoire
with leaves and berries*

*A pink armoire
with an open door
and open drawers*

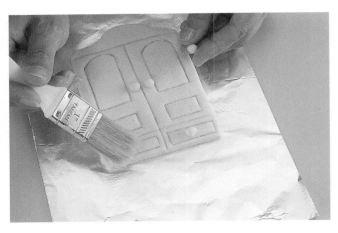

After having spread out the saltdough, cut out a rectangle ⅜" (1 cm) thick. With a pointed knife, draw the doors and drawers, and cut out the cornice.

Add the door and drawer knobs after having moistened them lightly with a brush.

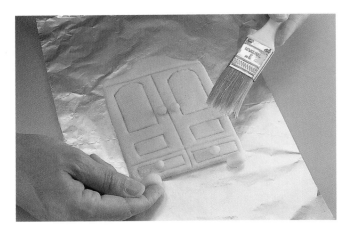

On the cornice, depending on the style of armoire your are creating (Normandy style, buffet, clothes closet, pantry, etc.) you can draw fruit and flowers.

Attach the feet by moistening the elements lightly.

🕐 Bake 1 hour at 200°F (100°C), then 2 hours at 250°F (125°C).

A grey and blue armoire

If you've never had the luck to inherit a grandfather's clock, or if you have never been able to buy yourself one, here is a chance to model your own.

Feed your inspiration by visiting art and craft museums, as well as going through magazines, searching in the library, postcards, brochures, or antique shops...

This way, in your spare time, you can study and observe the various styles and motifs.

🕐 Bake your creation for 1 hour at 200°F (100°C), then 30 minutes at 250°F (125°C).

The modeling is very simple. The most interesting work consists of decorating the clock, which lends itself admirably to primitive painting with flowers, vines, and symmetrical motifs.

Use a paint with good coverage, and lots of lively colors.

A pink and gray grandfather's clock

Bathrooms certainly lend themselves to white decors, but still they must be warm and welcoming. To accomplish this, you can add a bit of lace glued to the edge of the bathtub for a frilly effect. (See page 45.)

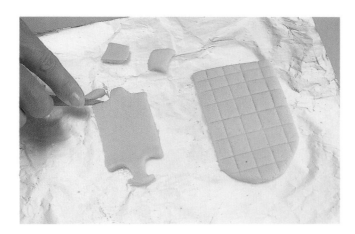

Roll out the saltdough in a shape rounded at the top. Then, using a knife, trace squares for ceramic tiles, vertically and horizontally. Cut out the shape shown above left and place it in the center of your title section, lightly moistening the area first.

Model a large ball of saltdough, then hollow it out. Your washbasin is ready. Trace under the edge using a knitting needle.

Model, then install the faucet.

🕐 Bake the piece for 1 hour at 200°F (100°C) so as to avoid any swelling, then bake 30 minutes longer at 250°F (125°C).

The attic is a fun place in which you can place all kinds of miniature objects made of saltdough: from dishes to books, rugs, a birdcage, baskets, wheat sacks, trunks…you can hang bouquets of dried flowers from the rafters, add some furniture…and why not, in addition to the cats, some rats, or an owl.

THE GRAIN SACKS

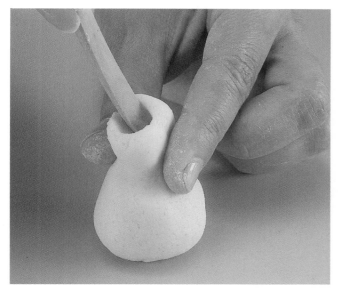

Model a large ball, then thin it towards the top. Hollow it with a tapered stick.

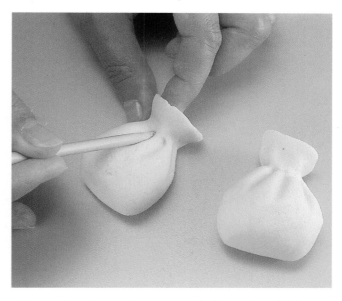

To make the sacks appear full, sculpt folds with a knitting needle.

 Bake.

After having painted and varnished the sack, tie a string or bit of raffia around the top.

The decoration of a jam cupboard requires just as much creativity and attention as the decoration of a Christmas tree. On this jam cupboard in the cats' attic, green acrylic paint brings out the water color used for the jam pots.

You can also add a dried bunch of garlic or red peppers.

Roll out the dough, and cut a rounded rectangle from it. Use a knife to trace a second rectangle inside this one. With the index finger, lightly press the inside of this rectangle.

Cut out two thin strips for the shelves.

Place them inside the jam cupboard.

Fasten them by moistening the elements with a brush.

Mark the cornices and groove the uprights of the piece, using a knitting needle.

Attach the cupboard feet.

Model the jam pots of different sizes.

Arrange them on the shelves and on the cornice.

SOME MORE IDEAS

THE CORNER CUPBOARD WITH CROCKERY

The wooden shelves are traced, then their grooves cut with a pointed knife. Place the shelves on the prebaked braces. Paint them with water color paint, then varnish them.

A bit of lace can be glued around the edges of the shelves. The little nails should be placed before baking.

THE TABLE

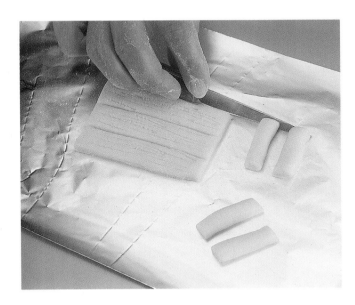

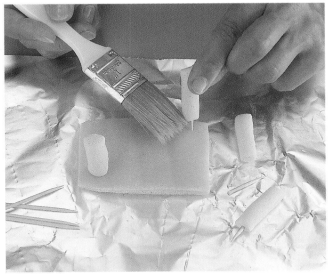

Cut out a rectangle of dough, then groove it with a knife blade.

Model four rolls of equal size.

 Bake for 10 minutes at 200°F (100°C).

Turn the table upside down. Place a toothpick in each roll, then attach a roll at each corner of the table.

 Bake for 1 hour at 200°F (100°C).

THE BENCH

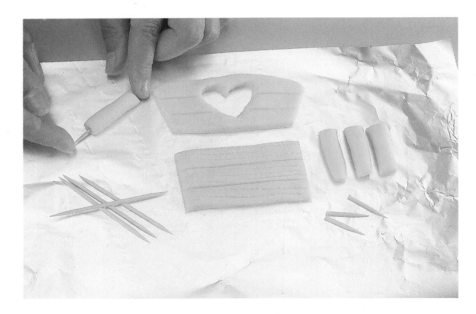

Cut out and groove the seat, then the back of the bench.

On the back, cut a heart in the center, then remove it.

Model and attach the four legs of the bench.

🕐 Bake the feet first for 10 minutes, then assemble and bake the bench for 1 hour at 200°F (100°C).

THE CHAIR

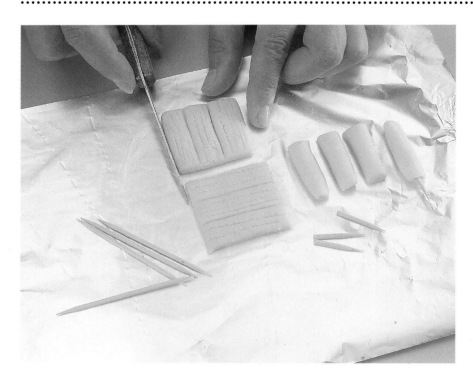

Cut out a rectangle of dough, groove it, then cut in two squares: one square for the seat, and one square for the back. Model the four legs, bake them, then attach them to the chair seat with toothpicks.

🕐 Bake the whole chair for 1 hour at 200°F (100°C).

Model all the elements of the dog. Insert a toothpick in the roll of the body so as to maintain the position of the head.

DISPLAYING YOUR DOLL FURNITURE

The marvelous miniature furniture you've created can be displayed in a number of ways. Group a few pieces on a shelf or a full-size end table, where they'll serve as delightful decorations and conversation starters. Use the pieces in a doll house that already exists.

Or, if you like, create a special doll house just for all the furniture you've made, using simple plywood and following the instructions below.

TIPS FOR SECURING THE FURNITURE

Of course, you don't want the furniture to tumble to the floor the first time somebody walks into your doll house. There are several ways to fasten the furniture safely to the house.

Before Baking
This technique works well for large, bulky pieces, such as armoires and jam cupboards. Buy a spool of steel wire (not too thick), which you can cut as needed with a pair of nippers. Cut off a fairly short piece of wire and bend it into a hairpin shape. Push one end partway into the back of the furniture, being careful not to go all the way through. The protruding side of the wire can be fastened to the back of the house.

After Baking, Painting, and Varnishing
Furniture with a flat back can be fastened to a wall of the dollhouse with wood glue or quick-setting glue. If you want to be able to move the furniture around, you can use strips of hook-and-loop tape to attach the back of the furniture to the house.

CONSTRUCTING THE DOLL HOUSE

On a piece of plywood, mark out all the pieces of the house, following the diagrams and measurements on the next four pages. Cut out all pieces with a scroll saw. Sand each piece and label it with the part name.

Try dry-fitting the various pieces together, to make sure they fit. Then glue the pieces together with wood glue, reinforcing the joints with nails.

Once the house is completely assembled, sand it evenly. Paint it with a good primer coat and let it dry. Sand it again as needed. Follow with two coats of paint in your choice of colors.

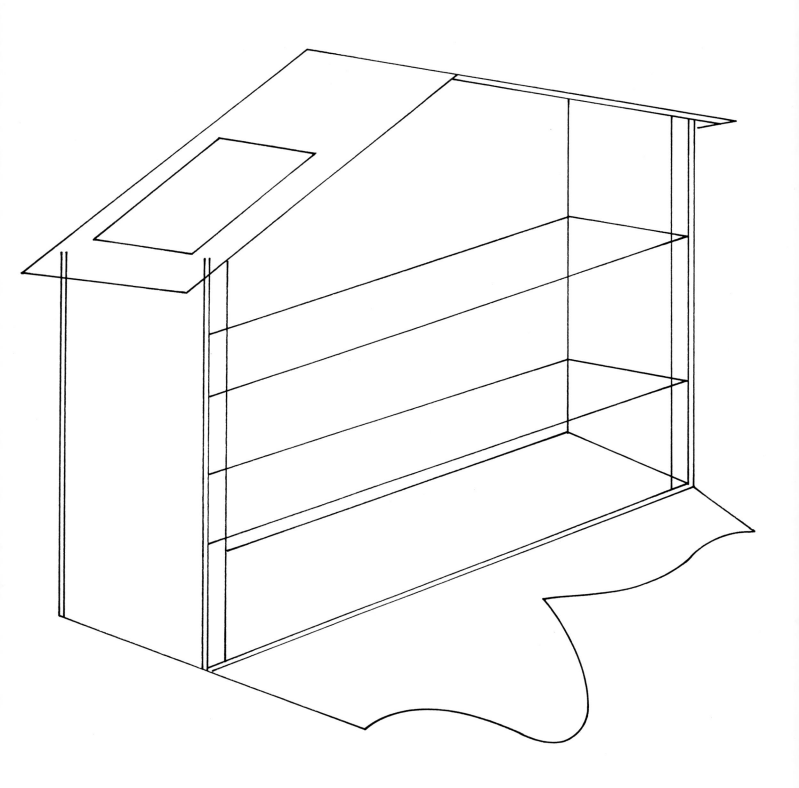

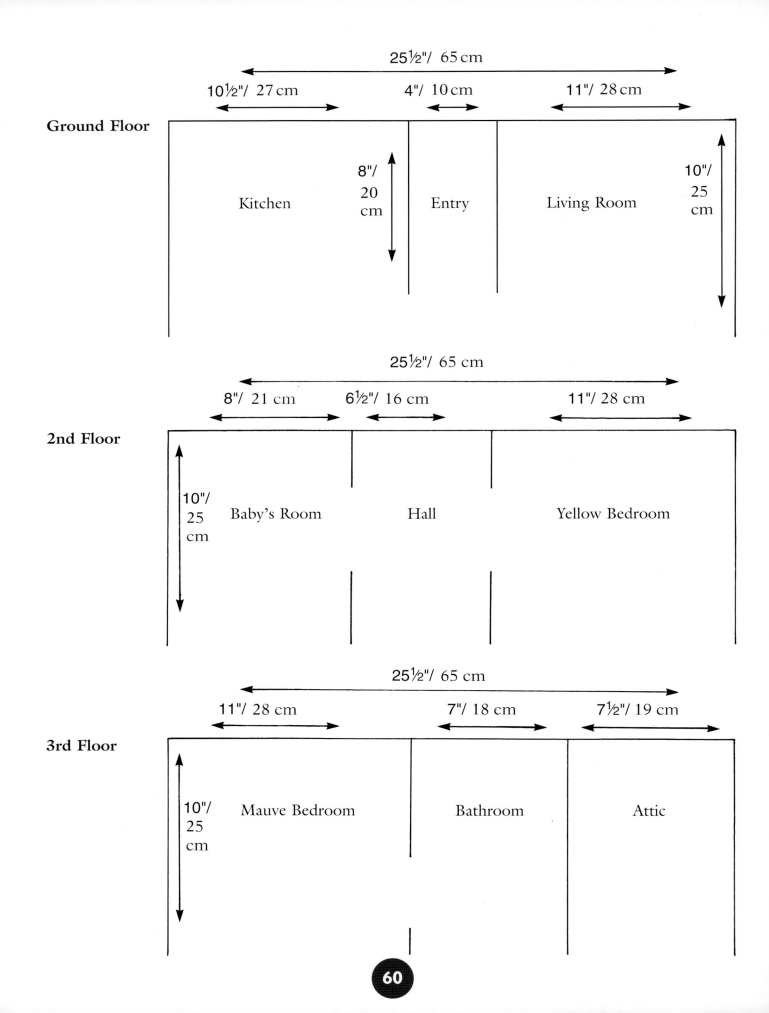

Ground Floor

25½"/ 65 cm

10½"/ 27 cm 4"/ 10 cm 11"/ 28 cm

Kitchen

8"/ 20 cm

Entry

Living Room

10"/ 25 cm

2nd Floor

25½"/ 65 cm

8"/ 21 cm 6½"/ 16 cm 11"/ 28 cm

10"/ 25 cm

Baby's Room

Hall

Yellow Bedroom

3rd Floor

25½"/ 65 cm

11"/ 28 cm 7"/ 18 cm 7½"/ 19 cm

10"/ 25 cm

Mauve Bedroom

Bathroom

Attic

**The Roof,
right and
left sides**

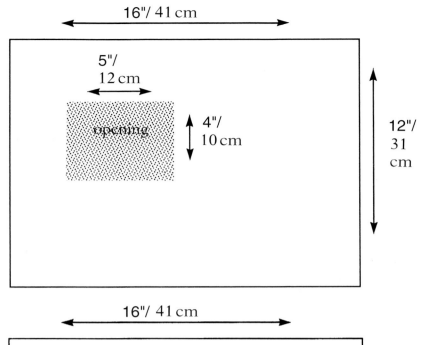

16"/ 41 cm

5"/
12 cm

opening

4"/
10 cm

12"/
31
cm

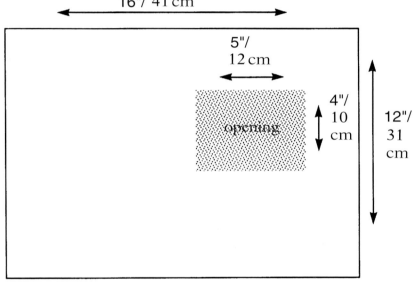

16"/ 41 cm

5"/
12 cm

opening

4"/
10
cm

12"/
31
cm

**The Walls,
right and
left sides
(cut 2)**

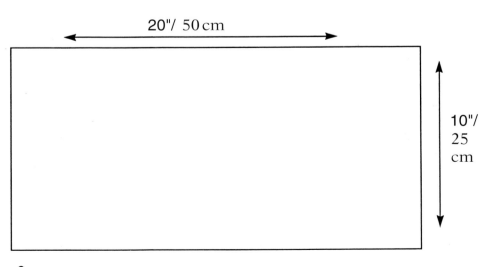

20"/ 50 cm

10"/
25
cm

x 2

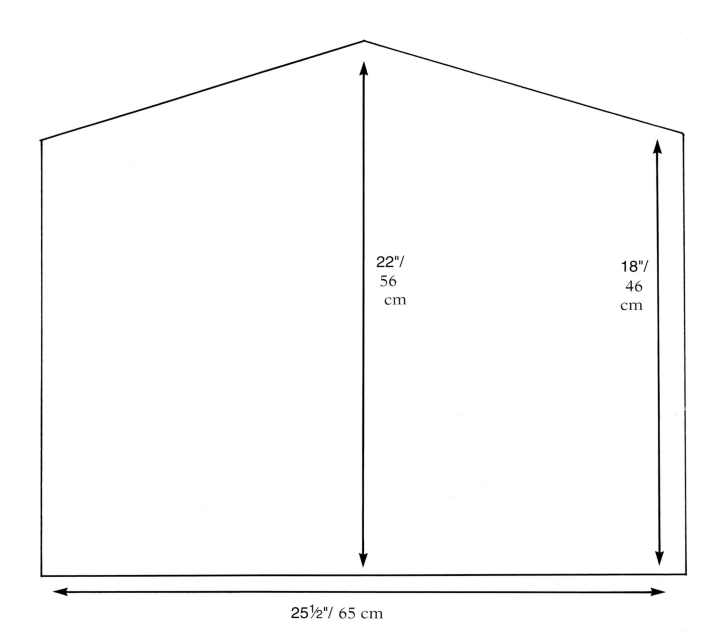

22"/
56
cm

18"/
46
cm

25½"/ 65 cm

TABLE DECORATIONS

SPRING

Titmouse wreath

Hide the synthetic moss under the natural moss.

Arrange the leaves and flowers.

These hearts are fastened on a ribbon with a strong glue.

Intersperse the hearts, if you wish, with the star anise.

You can color them with curry or paprika. As these spices have a strong and agreeable fragrance, the hearts will be welcome in the kitchen. So do not varnish them, as this would inhibit the spread of their scent. Hang them on a cabinet door or window latch.

Certain cabbages can serve up quite a surprise! If you're not sure how to tell him what you're about to find under a cabbage leaf, prepare a pretty table and place these cabbage babies on his plate to announce the happy event. That should liven up the table talk for the rest of the evening.

Procure a coarsely textured cabbage. Remove the large leaves, wash and dry them.

Once the saltdough is rolled out, lay a cabbage leaf on it and imprint it on the dough, by pressing with the palm of your hand or a rolling pin. Cut out cabbage leaf shapes.

Place a sheet of aluminum foil inside a heat-resistant bowl. Lay the saltdough leaves in the bowl, one overlapping the other, until there are several layers. Set the baby, the twins, or even triplets in place, and tuck them in with the cabbage leaves.

🕐 This creation is relatively thick, so it may be baked for two hours in the bowl at 200°F (100°C). Then, remove the aluminum foil and the bowl, and bake at 250°F (125°C) for 3 more hours.

BIRTHDAY CANDLEHOLDERS

Two mauve blossoms for two year olds

Five pink blossoms for five year olds

With modeled letters, you can decorate names and messages: for Saint Valentine's day, for parties, a Happy Birthday, I love you, Happy New Year, Home Sweet Home, etc. You'll enjoy other people's delight in these one-of-a-kind gifts.

Such letters can also let you designate your guests' places at the table. They are easy enough to make with thick strands of dough, or better yet cut them out with custom cookie cutters. Coordinate the colors with those of the table cloth and napkins.

With decorated letters, you can create a multitude of gifts and original games. To do this, roll some saltdough to a thickness of ⅜" (1 cm) on your floured work surface. You can use cookie cutters or sand molds to cut out the letters by pressing through the dough. Letters and figures are available in craft stores. To keep the molds from distorting the shapes when they are removed, you should sprinkle them with flour so they will detach easily. Place the letters on aluminum foil or on a cookie sheet and bake them at 200°F (100°C) for 30 minutes, then remove the support and place them directly on the middle rack in the oven. Continue baking at the same temperature for 30 minutes.

AN EASTER BUNNY

One of the more delightful icons of springtime, this is modeled using the same techniques as other similar figures in this book. Use toothpicks to join ears, head, feet, and the eggs. The arms, torso, and legs are reinforced with two hairpin-shaped wires.

CORN CANDLEHOLDER

Prepare the base. As with all the candleholders, the base is molded by hand and placed on aluminum foil. Wrap the bottom of the candle with foil, and press it into the base. Remove the candle, leaving the foil in place during subsequent baking.

Next, make the five ears of corn. Once the cobs are formed, arrange three shucks, which are scored with a pointed knife. Arrange them on aluminum foil, slightly moistened, and add little balls (kernels) of saltdough. Add the stem, cut from a coil, and score it.

Fashion the candleholder base (as on the previous page).

Decorate the periphery of the base with leaves and strawberries.

The strawberry basket must be filled with a sheet of aluminum foil, making sure that it follows the contours of the basket. Cover it fully with leaves and strawberries.

Bake it for about two hours at 200°F (100°C) with the basket. Remove the aluminum foil and set the basket aside. Continue baking at 250°F (125°C) until it is dried thoroughly.

To complete your decoration, you can also arrange leaves and strawberries, grouped or not, around the candleholder.

Basket of yellow flowers and daisies

Basket of yellow plums

Arranged on a table with children's snacks, these cakes can be used to help seat your little guests. So why not complete the baker's tray, and offer one to each child.

Better yet, why not make these tiny treats part of the party by allowing each child to make his or her own cake? Simply arrange a table with a variety of pre-cut dough shapes such as balls, leaves, candlesticks, round layers, and base shapes, along with bowls of water and paintbrushes, and let each child's birthday cake fantasies run wild. You might want to consider shifting the cake decorations to more kid-friendly items such as animals or sports balls, but keep the shapes simple, for your sake and your young guests'. Tiny fingers may need help attaching some of the smaller pieces, such as candlesticks and flames, and adult guidance should always be used during the baking stage. Finally, be sure to have plenty of newspaper on hand for the painting process! Their cakes may not turn out as neatly manicured as our examples, but your little guests' creations are sure to be just as delectable and full of charm. Best of all, they're guaranteed to have them smiling with delight by party's end—especially when they get to carry their fantasy cakes home with them! (Note: Explain to children that dough creations are for decoration only, and should not be eaten.)

Roll out logs of saltdough and form some into rings. You only need to hide the napkin ring joint and cover it with some fruit, vegetables, or flowers made from saltdough.

These pretty articles of tableware will increase the pleasure of a children's snack, by associating the enjoyability of the presentation with the variety of the food.

Very simple to create, they can even be made by the children themselves.

A WOODLAND CENTERPIECE

Spread out the saltdough to an ample thickness. This mass will serve as a support which will give volume to your creation from the start. To reduce baking time, you can mold a more uniform thickness of dough over a wad of aluminum foil. Next, reserve the place for the nest with a ball of aluminum foil, which will remain in the dough until the modeling is finished. After varnishing you will be able to install the nest there.

Cut out some leaves of various shapes from the dough, and place them on the support to hide it. Model the apples and mushrooms. Arrange more leaves. Vary your decor by integrating some nuts and berries. Fill in any empty spaces with leaves.

This creation should be painted with watercolor only, to give more depth and softness, then varnished with a matte varnish. The nest should be glued on, along with little candles in the shape of eggs.

CANDLEHOLDER OF OAK LEAVES AND ACORNS

Create a base as described previously. Then decorate it by alternating oak leaves and acorns. Being relatively thick, this model must be baked for five hours at 250°F (125°C). It should be painted with water colors only, then coated with matte varnish.

This model is created just like the one before. The plums and elderberries alternate and are overlapped with their respective leaves.

🕐 Baking time is about five hours at 250°F (125°C).

HOLLY AND ALDER SEEDS WREATH

Find a wreath form made of synthetic foam. It can be bought in a craft store, or from a florist. Cover the wreath form with natural moss, then insert your saltdough decorations into it with wires or wooden picks.

Spray the piece with sparkle finish.

WREATH OF MOSS WITH RED FLOWERS

This wreath base should be made of straw. Cover it entirely with a natural moss; hold the moss in place by wrapping transparent fishing line around the base.

Let it dry several days in the open air, but not in the sun; the moss should stay fresh and green.

Insert some little flowers made from saltdough. The more numerous they are, the more festive the wreath will be. Add some candles in varied forms and colors. You could also add some pine cone candles. Finish it off with ribbons.

Make two coils and braid them into a wreath 8" (20 cm) in diameter. Place it on aluminum foil. Push down four places for candles at regular intervals. Between these places, add apples, leaves and musical instruments that you will have modeled carefully.

For example, to create the lyre, model a coil which you curve back at each end. Then make some straight coils and set them close together to resemble strings. A last coil will be laid horizontally across the others to hold the assembly together. After baking, paint the instruments with acrylic paints.

Clear varnish should be used to preserve the saltdough. Every year, revarnish the wreath and, of course, change the candles.

This angel was modeled following a concert given in a baroque church. Baroque art is an art of movement and color which should, if you like it, give you many rich ideas for the holidays.

The column used here is rather simple. You can multiply it, for example, by placing three angels on it.

Creating this type of motif will allow you to reproduce a detail of antique furniture, or better still, the scroll of a mandolin, a lute, or a viola.

Different shades of gold can be used.

Excercise good control over your painting so
that you leave no surface untouched by color.

Angels will lend gaiety to your Christmas table.

You can decorate your table throughout December with motifs lending an air of celebration. So why wait for the 24th or 25th when you can prolong the festivities!

These little angels are lightweight and bake quickly, from an hour to an hour and a half at 250°F (125°C). Baking must be adapted to the thickness and format of the modeling.

CHRISTMAS CONE WITH BUTTERFLIES, HEARTS, AND MUSHROOMS

Every butterfly, every heart and every mushroom is mounted on a thin metal wire. The red strawflowers are left in small bunches and stuck in a foam cone with a butterfly or a mushroom of saltdough mixed in. Fill in the empty spaces with loops of ribbon until the cone is entirely hidden.

Christmas Decorations

You can create many wreaths, objects to hang on Christmas trees, napkin holders and other table decorations using an unusual tool: the potter's syringe.

You can find this type of syringe, with many tips, in all stores specializing in potter's equipment.

Here are several designs which are easy to create. All you need to do is change the tip of the syringe to get different textures and thicknesses. Then you will have many variations to change the appearance of your saltdough creations, on which you will later add fruits, flowers, pine cones, leaves, and more.

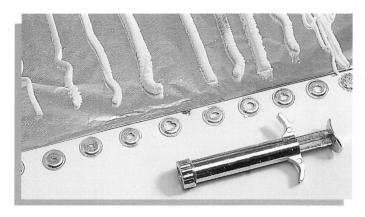

All you need to do is press the dough through your chosen tip. Press two thick strands of dough, then weave them from the middle to form a wreath. See holly wreaths, hearts, stars and a double heart on pages that follow.

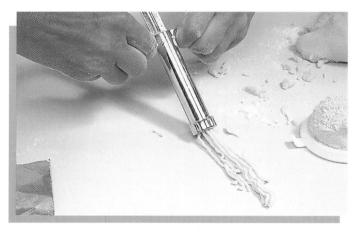

🕐 Baking time depends on the size of the piece. Times are given individually throughout most of these projects.

SIMPLE WREATHS

Start by modeling a large circle, which should be placed on aluminum foil. Then flatten it with the palm of your hand.

Decorate it with whatever objects you've chosen for your design.

WREATHS WITH TWO STRANDS

If you are braiding a wreath with two strands of dough, they should be the same length and width.

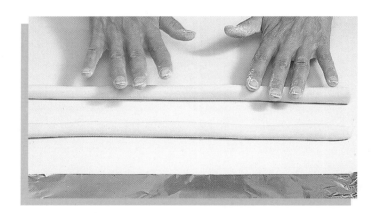

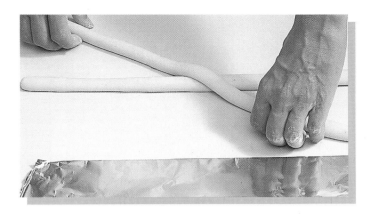

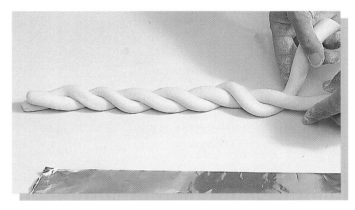

Lay them on aluminum foil, crossing them in the middle, and then braiding them. Always braid from the middle to the ends.

It is important to follow this technique, and not start to braid from the ends.

The braid will thus be more regular, and there will be no risk of the dough tearing.

Form the wreath.

Cut it at a right angle, with a knife, at both ends.

Moisten, then join the two ends.

You can then add to and decorate your wreath as you wish by adding fruit and leaves, or inserting other objects.

See the twins in a wreath, oranges and lemons, baby Jesus, and hearts and flowers on pages that follow.

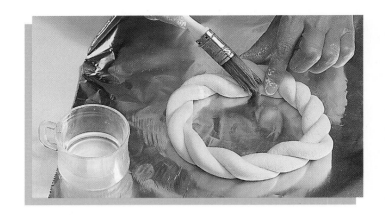

WREATHS WITH THREE STRANDS

Model three rolls with identical thickness and length.

Braid them, starting at the middle, always working toward the ends in a regular manner.

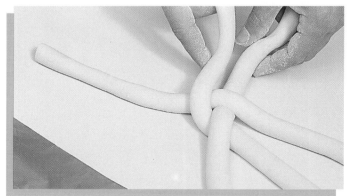

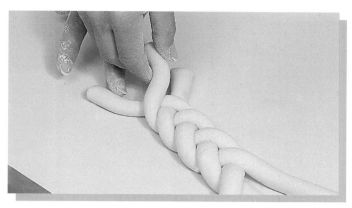

Your wreath will only be successful if the three strands remain strictly regular.

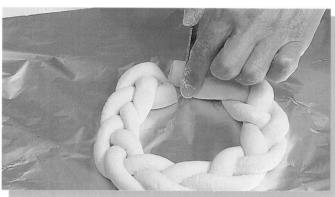

Cut both ends at right angles, moisten them at the junction with a brush, and join them securely.

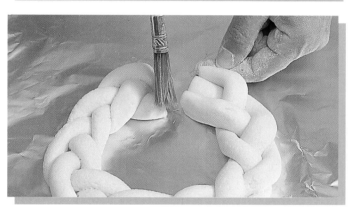

🕐 Most three-strand wreaths are relatively thick, and must be baked for 3 hours overall.

Bake them for 1 hour at 200°F (100°C), then remove the aluminum foil. Continue the baking at 250°F (125°C) for 2 hours.

HOLLY WREATHS

These simple little designs, decorated with a ribbon, can be placed on guest's plates, or on a straw knife holder, a gilded candlestick, or a festive tablecloth…inviting everyone to the evening's festivities.

Use a potter's syringe to press out the first length of dough, then bring the threads together.

Press out a second identical length. Braid them, always from the middle.

Form the first wreath on aluminum foil.

Repeat this procedure for the second wreath, this time smaller, and fit it in the middle of the first one.

Cut out some holly leaves with a cookie cutter, and place them on the wreath, moistening the parts to be joined. The two wreaths must be covered at the same places with the leaves and berries, which strengthens them and joins the wreaths together.

🕐 This wreath is open to the air, so its cooking time will be short: 1 hour and 30 minutes. Place it in the oven for 1 hour at 200°F (100°C), remove the aluminum foil, then continue baking for 30 minutes at 250°F (125°C).

DOUBLE HEART WREATH

Use a potter's syringe to press out four lengths of dough: two long ones for the exterior, and two short ones for the inside of the wreath. Give it the form of a heart on aluminum foil, and join them with leaves and little pine cones pressed into the saltdough.

WREATH WITH HEARTS AND STARS

Begin as you did for the holly wreath by pressing out two lengths of dough, which are then braided and joined together by light moistening.

Arrange the hearts and stars, made with a cookie cutter, alternating them and joining them by moistening with a brush.

Bake 1 hour and 30 minutes in all. Place in the oven for 1 hour at 200°F (100°C), remove the aluminum foil, then continue baking for 30 minutes at 250°F (125°C).

TWINS IN A WREATH

This is a wreath braided with two strands of dough.

Model and position two identical twins. Each little girl has an arm which rests on the wreath, as though she were leaning out of a window.

🕐 Bake 3 hours total: 1 hour at 200°F (100°C), then 2 hours at 250°F (125°C).

After painting and applying a matte varnish over the whole work, glue a little lace around the neck of each twin.

WREATH OF ORANGES AND LEMONS

The wreath is braided, then formed on a sheet of aluminum foil.

The holly leaves are formed with a cookie cutter.

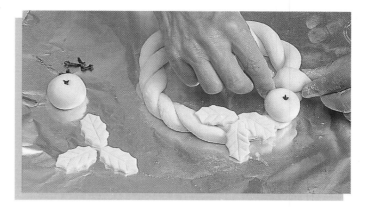

Apples and oranges are modeled, then a clove is put in the top.

They are arranged on the circle of the wreath by alternating fruits with holly leaves.

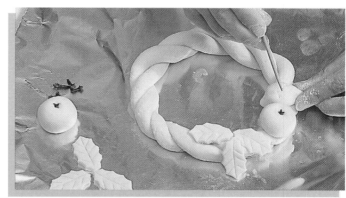

Once they are arranged on the wreath, be careful not to distort the fruits. You can stick them with a pin to mark the grain of the orange peel.

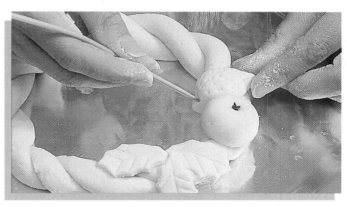

Don't forget to add the holly berries.

BABY JESUS

The wreath is formed with two strands. Let it bake while you model and place the little Jesus on the nest of straw, which is pressed through a sieve.

Bake in the oven for 15 minutes at 200°F (100°C), then arrange the decorations around the wreath with light moistening. Let the assembled model bake for 1 hour and 30 minutes at 250°F (125°C).

Why not decorate your wreaths with leaves and hearts formed with a cookie cutter? You need two or three leaves for each heart.

Using a kitchen knife, score the leaves to make the veins.

Arrange the lightly moistened leaves, then the hearts, around the wreath.

🕐 Bake for 2 hours and 30 minutes in all. Place in the oven for 1 hour at 200°F (100°C), remove the aluminum foil, then continue the baking for 1 hour and 30 minutes at 250°F (125°C).

WREATH OF HEARTS AND MUSHROOMS

WREATH OF FRUITS AND PINE CONES

It's a good idea to wash the pine cones first, then dry them. This will avoid getting dirt on your brush during varnishing.

Insert the pine cones by pressing them slightly into the saltdough. They will be baked with the wreath and thus will firmly retain their position.

This wreath is painted entirely with a transparent type of ink. It is then varnished. The alder berries are glued in place, then lightly whitened with gouache.

SIMPLE CANDLEHOLDERS

Roll some saltdough to a thickness of ¼" (0.6 cm), then cut out some shapes with a round form. Surround the candles with aluminum foil and press them into the saltdough.

Remove the candle, but leave its imprint with the aluminum foil.

Moisten the full surface of each candle holder and position some decorations cut out in the shapes of hearts, stars, shamrocks, etc.

SMALL GILDED CANDLEHOLDERS

These are identical to the simple candleholders. But in this case, we have a decoration based on a repetition of leaves cut out with the cookie cutter.

The candleholders are then painted with different kinds of yellow or reddish gold acrylic paint.

Displayed with green, red, or white candles amidst the full spread of a holiday table, or even in a simple setting, gilded saltdough candleholders add an elegant and handcrafted touch to the atmosphere that will keep your guests in the dark about how easy they were to make. If you're looking for a scented addition to your holiday decor, consider revising the base of the candleholders to accomodate votive candles. Simply use a larger round form to cut out your dough and follow the same steps, using a votive candle 2" or 3" (5 or 7.5 cm) tall to form the impression in the dough. A votive candleholder may require more leaves and cutouts to cover the surface, as well. Placed around your home on coffee tables and mantlepieces, votives scented with pine, cranberry, or cinnamon will bring out the holiday spirit in every room. Be sure to keep an eye on your festive scents and sparkling lights, however. It's a good idea to check your candles periodically to prevent wax from dripping onto the candleholders.

Model the body of the basket, with a thickness of ¾"-1¼" (2-3 cm), on aluminum foil. Then place the handle shaped from two woven strands, attaching them on each side of the basket. Score the basket body with the point of a knife.

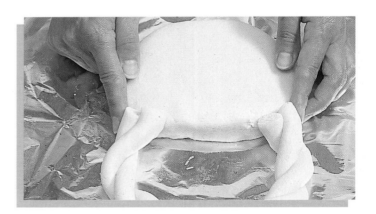

Then, using two forks held tine-to-tine, press on the weave of the basket.

This procedure must be repeated over every part of the basket.

Then add some leaves, apples, and a bunch of grapes.

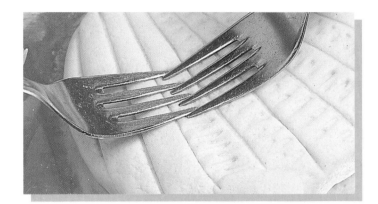

As this model is rather thick, it must be baked for 4 hours and 30 minutes in all. Place in the oven for 1 hour and 30 minutes, remove the aluminum foil, and prolong the cooking for 3 hours at 250°F (125°C).

When cool, the basket is varnished with two layers of gold sparkle spray.

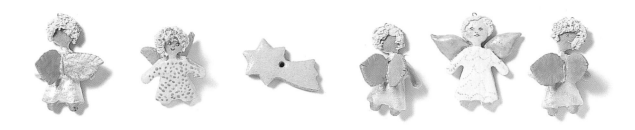

MOBILE OF STARS AND ANGELS

The angels are cut out with cookie cutters, using a saltdough ¼" (0.6 cm) thick. Shape the wings by cutting them out with a knife.

Use a cookie cutter to cut the moons, the simple stars, hollowed stars, and shooting stars of different sizes and shapes. Don't forget to pierce them with a straw so you can thread a string to hang the mobile. Cooking time for the cutout pieces is 1 hour at 200°F (100°C).

Bake the wings for 10 minutes at 200°F (100°C), then remove them from the oven. Let them cool, and fasten them to the backs of the angels with a little piece of aluminum. Don't forget to insert a hook of twisted steel wire in the head of each angel. Then replace them in the oven for 40 minutes at 250°F (125°C).

Painting: You will find several choices of shades of gold in acrylic paints. The figures should be painted on both sides.

Supplies: A straw wreath about 14" (36 cm) in diameter, fresh moss, ivy, transparent fishing line, ribbon, a pair of scissors, and straight pins.

Cover the wreath entirely with moss, holding it in place with the fishing line, which you will wind around the wreath, totally covering the straw. Then surround the wreath with strands of ivy, fastened with pins. Cut the ribbon into three or four strips of equal length, and knot them together. You will thus be able to fasten your wreath above the table or to a beam. Install your saltdough figures with the fishing line, one after the other, being careful to keep your mobile in balance.

CUCKOO CLOCK

Roll out the saltdough on your slightly-floured working surface. Then cut the bottom of the cuckoo clock, the roof (composed of two rectangular slopes), then two rectangular sides, and finally a little base on which you trace the paving stones with a knife. Use a cookie cutter to cut out some holly leaves, and model some small uniform balls to serve as berries. Insert two hooks in the bottom of the clock to fasten the two children.

🕐 Bake for 2 hours in all. Place the different pieces in the oven for 1 hour at 200°F (100°C). Then assemble all the cuckoo clock elements by moistening them lightly each time. Place the assembled clock in the oven, and bake for 1 hour at 250°F (125°C).

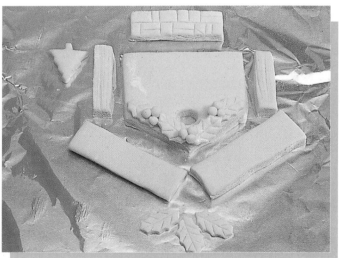

THE COTTAGE

Roll the saltdough to a thickness of ⅜"
(1 cm). Cut out the facade of the cottage,
design the position of the windows, then
remove the centers. Trace the door, then score
it with a knife. Assemble the chimney, the first
slope of the roof and then the second, moistening each time.

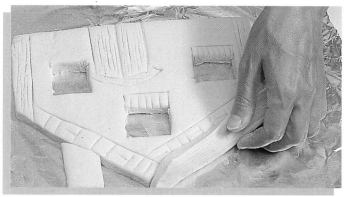

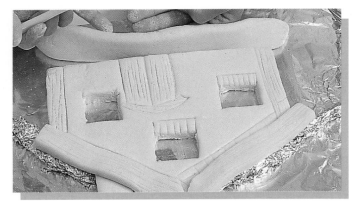

Place a strip of flat saltdough in front of the cottage to make a sidewalk. Moisten it and join it to the cottage. Then arrange the shutter, the Christmas decorations around the windows, the letter box, the snow, the two birds, etc.

🕐   As in the case of the basket, this is a fairly large work. It must be baked at least 3 hours: 1 hour at 200°F (100°C), remove the aluminum foil, then continue baking for 2 hours at 250°F (125°C).

If the model does not seem perfectly dry, continue the baking for another half hour.

Here is an amusing creation. We are used to seeing Santa Claus dashing around, but this time he's decided to grab a minute of well-deserved rest.

Start with the body of the sleigh, cut out from a piece of saltdough ⅜" (1 cm) thick, around which you will place two braided coils, cut with a knife. Model two feet of equal dimensions, and set in place.

🕐 Bake for 4 hours in all. In the first phase, bake for 1 hour at 200°F (100°C), remove the aluminum foil, and put back in the oven for 3 hours at 250°F (125°C).

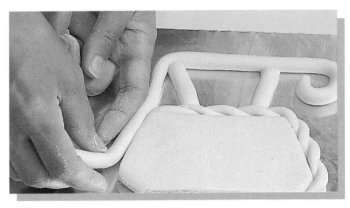

Roll a coil to form the runner and install it, curled back at both ends.

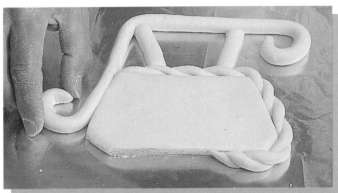

Always moistening, continue to assemble the model, following the accompanying photographs.

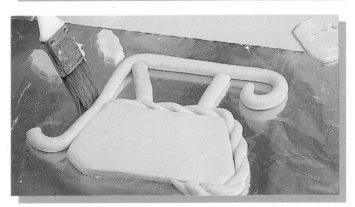

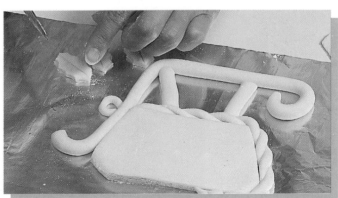

Score some holly leaves and arrange them, with their berries, along the sleigh runners.

Model the head and body of Santa Claus. Install him, lying down on the sleigh.

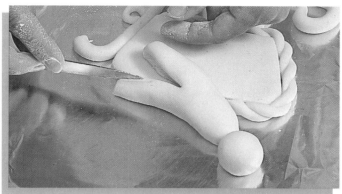

Score his trousers with a knife.

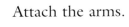

Attach the arms.

Arrange the blanket, then the down comforter, after pinching the corners.

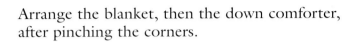

Bring the arms out over the comforter.

Set the hood in place.

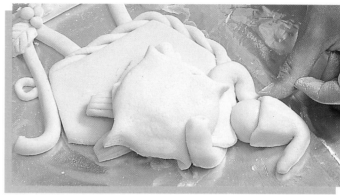

Add the pom-pom and hair, using saltdough squeezed through a sieve.

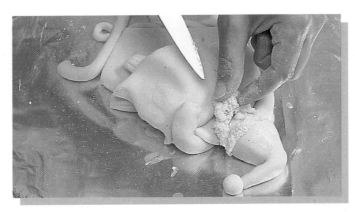

Place a collar around his neck.

Model a little round nose.

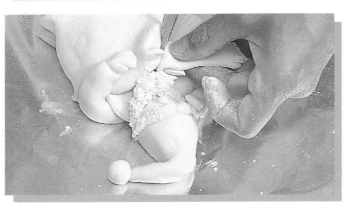

Add the fringed scarf and the mittens.

THE CHRISTMAS STOCKING

For children and adults, Christmas is the merriest holiday of the whole year. The long wait, preparations, the excitement through the house, from kitchen to attic—everything incites a dream and increases the impatience of the children as each day passes. Then the evening comes to hang stockings near the chimney....

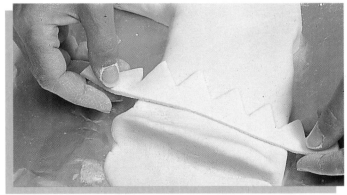

Spread the saltdough with the palm of your hand on aluminum foil, and give it the shape of a stocking.

Still using the palm of your hand, hollow the top, which will be used to support the decorative pieces.

Place a strip of dough as shown, then adjust it and cut it out to the measurement of the stocking.

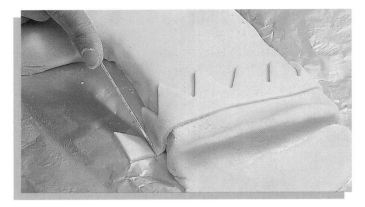

Model some balls, and arrange them as sleigh-bells, one by one, around the stocking, moistening them slightly.

Next, arrange the toys inside the top, moistening each time you add one. Crowd the toys against each other. Then the stocking will be full, and what an effect it will create!

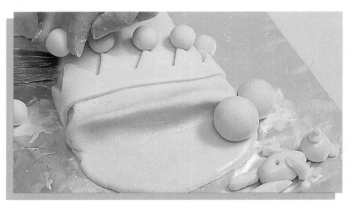

🕐 This modeling will need 6 hours of baking: 1 hour at 200°F (100°C), then 5 hours at 250°F (125°C).

It is then painted with acrylic, followed by a high-gloss varnish.

SNOWMAN WITH TREES

Shape the balls needed for the snowman by rolling the saltdough in the palm of the hand. One should be 2¼" (6 cm) in diameter, and the other 1½" (4 cm) in diameter (approximately). Join these securely for the body and head, then form and attach the arms.

Make sure the parts stick together by moistening them and pressing them together lightly. Model small balls for the nose and buttons. Complete the creation with a hat and scarf. Add the trees, stars, and holly, then insert some hooks to suspend your creation.

🕐 Bake for 2 hours total: 1 hour at 200°F (100°C), then 1 hour at 250°F (125°C).

PLAIN MEDALLIONS

Roll out some saltdough on your floured working surface to a thickness of ¼" (0.6 cm). Using a cookie cutter, cut the ornaments from the dough. Make one or two small holes with a straw in one edge, depending on the format of the medallions.

Using small cookie cutters, cut out some decorations to add to the medallions. Moisten the medallions with a pastry brush, and add the decorations.

🕐 Bake for 2 hours total: 1 hour at 200°F (100°C) to prevent the formation of bubbles, then 1 hour at 250°F (125°C).

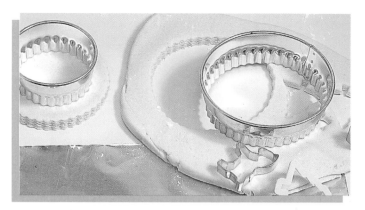

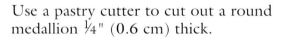

Use a pastry cutter to cut out a round medallion ¼" (0.6 cm) thick.

Using a smaller pastry cutter, remove the center. Place the hollow medallion on aluminum foil. Bend it into an oval shape.

Arrange the decorative cut-outs around the medallion, moistening them slightly. Using a straw, pierce the medallion at two places, so that after varnishing you can slip a ribbon through it and hang it.

🕐 Bake for 2 hours total: 1 hour at 200°F (100°C) to prevent the formation of bubbles, then 1 hour at 250°F (125°C).

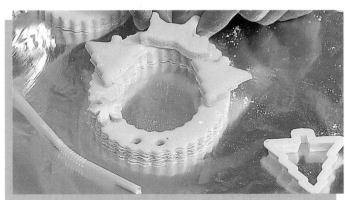

PASTRY CUTTER ORNAMENTS

It was while traveling in France and abroad that I collected my pastry cutters. They are usually made of stainless steel or plastic, and have many variations. All through the month of December, you can be creating your Christmas cookies and decorations to please both old and young.

During this holiday season, you can cut and paint golden giraffes, ponies, bears, rabbits, geese, trolls, and mushrooms all from salt-dough, which will join the hearts, stars and traditional angels for decorating the Christmas tree.

Cut your objects from a sheet ¼" (0.6 cm) thick, using pastry cutters, varying the forms and sizes. You can then gild them with egg yoke, or paint them and varnish both sides after baking. You can also add a sparkled varnish spray if you like.

Some advice: Wash your stainless steel pastry cutters well in soapy water, because the salt can damage them and they can rust easily. Dry them thoroughly with a dish towel, or better still, put them in an oven that is still hot before putting them away. That will allow them to dry completely.

GARLANDS

Using either pastry cutters or just freehand modeling, make a quantity of hearts, Christmas trees, and stars which you will paint and varnish on both sides. You can fasten them to a red or green cord, sewing or tying them on, one by one.

PLAYING CARD TAGS

Christmas is a season of secrets. No one must know what is hidden in the packages hidden in the closets. It's fun to make packages, to choose the papers and ribbons, and to write on a card tag the name that identifies each package.

These cards are modeled after playing cards. We need only to pierce them to be able to attach them to the gifts.

Supplies: Plywood, paper and crayons, a sabre saw, 1 small pot of paint, 1 wall hook, 48 small flat-head nails.

According to the design you want, use the sabre saw to cut a Christmas tree or some other shape from the plywood. Sand it if necessary. Give it a coat of green paint and let it dry. Attach a hook in the back to hang it on the wall.

Then hammer the 48 nails in rows, half on the tree and half on the base.

Prepare 24 little hanging figures with wire loops at the top. Hang them on the base, and paint numbers on the tree.

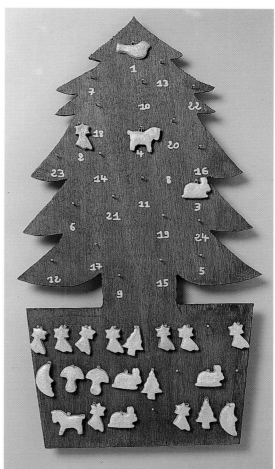

INDEX